SMALL SCENES
FROM A BIG GALAXY

VESA LEHTIMÄKI

For Aku

SMALL SCENES
FROM A BIG GALAXY

VESA LEHTIMÄKI

DK | Penguin Random House

CONTENTS

FOREWORD

In the LEGO® *Star Wars*® development team, we do our best to stimulate children's creativity and imagination with our products. However, over the years, we have also seen how the LEGO *Star Wars* universe has achieved the same for adult fans of the franchise. For us, it is always fun and exciting to see the creative ways in which both children and adults enjoy LEGO *Star Wars*.

The book you hold in your hands right now is a fantastic example of this.

Vesa Lehtimäki's work is certainly FUN and EXCITING—an important part of the LEGO *Star Wars* DNA. Vesa adds a completely new dimension to LEGO *Star Wars*, with an incredible level of authenticity that really brings the models and minifigures to life.

On top of this, Vesa Lehtimäki is a fantastic photographer, which makes this book a true piece of art. His work is sure to inspire LEGO *Star Wars* fans of all ages.

Jens Kronvold Frederiksen
LEGO Design Director

Louise Weiss Borup
LEGO Marketing Manager

Vesa Lehtimäki, also known by the internet alias Avanaut, is an illustrator and toy photographer. His LEGO®Star Wars® themed photographs have featured in many publications and websites, such as *Wired, ABC, Stern, Mashable, Buzzfeed, NBC Today,* and *The Huffington Post*. Vesa's work with LEGO photography also had an influence on the look of THE LEGO® MOVIE™ (2014). The image that regularly accompanies his online work is on the opposite page. Vesa is married, lives in Helsinki, Finland, and likes movies.

flickr.com/photos/avanaut   instagram.com/avanaut   twitter.com/TheAvanaut   facebook.com/avanaut

INTRODUCTION

The first *Star Wars* film in 1977 was the game changer. It just blew my eleven-year-old mind. I fell in love with the droids, spaceships, stormtroopers—everything that was designed for that movie. I rediscovered *Star Wars* in 2009 when I decided to document my son's toys before they vanished or were given away. When I began shooting the LEGO® *Star Wars*® toys, I realized I still had a personal connection to the stories and designs. *Star Wars* came back to me.

Before long, I discovered that there was a whole world of toy photography and began creating and uploading my own online. I am from Finland, so I naturally wanted to combine snow and blizzards with LEGO minifigures. I was especially inspired to create scenes set on the planet Hoth, as seen in *Star Wars:* Episode V *The Empire Strikes Back*. However, instead of just recreating scenes from that movie, I wanted to create my own, featuring the maintenance crews, the anonymous pilots and other background characters going about their business, not just on Hoth, but on Endor and Tatooine, too. Some photographs featured main characters, but always outside the movies' events.

For instance, Darth Vader doesn't listen to bossa nova in the movies, but in my photographs he does —he even wears pajamas under his armor! Soon, short scenarios became an integral part of my photographs. I felt as if I was writing, staging, directing, and shooting little one-frame movie scenes in the *Star Wars* universe that were completely my own. I loved that. I still do.

I stayed within the original *Star Wars* trilogy because that's what I know best. It's also because, originally, I borrowed all the LEGO models from my son. I wanted to limit my work so that he could enjoy the rest of his toys in peace!

I made a little book of my LEGO *Star Wars* Hoth photographs as a birthday present for him a few years ago. It was not available to the public. I never thought that my photographs would actually end up in a book in real life, certainly not in a big, lavish one like this. This is a dream come true. This book makes me look at my eleven-year-old self with a big, big smile.

However, I do not see my photographs as just for children. They are for adults, too. There is playful humor there, but in order to appreciate some of the photographs you need to be a little older than eleven! Perhaps they are for the child that, hopefully, resides somewhere in us all.

Vesa Lehtimäki, Helsinki, 2015

TATOOINE

The desert planet of Tatooine is a bone-dry world of dunes, rocks, and sudden sandstorms. It is here that the loathsome Jabba the Hutt holds court. However, even he has little control over the fierce Tusken Raiders and scavenging Jawas.

Rough Tatooine Landings • The idea behind this image was that X-wings were not suited to Tatooine's rough terrain. In order to get this shot, I dropped the model from about half a meter (1 ft 8 in) and photographed it as it bounced, so that the "sand" flew upward.

>> Pages 12–13 **Figrin D'an and the Modal Nodes Featuring Max Rebo** • I imagined that Max liked to hang around with cool players and was too good to waste his talent in that mediocre show band at Jabba's. I used a toy smoke machine to create atmosphere in the shot.

" This is for my next album cover! "

Max Rebo • This portrait was tricky to create because of reflections, so I shot through semi-transparent paper to diffuse the light. I lit Max from above and below using LED torches. I used a bit of Photoshop to improve the focus on the eyes.

"What do you mean, you're fresh out of blue milk?"

The Thing With the Blue Milk • I imagined that the Tusken Raiders were too hooked on blue milk...I've tried to get this to work many times. The reflections from a live laser beam make the camera sensor go awry—it just cannot read the parallel waves of laser light coming at it—and as a result the reflections appear as noise. Either I had to accept that, or choose to Photoshop the beam in. I really wanted the beam to be real, hence the noisy reflections.

"I like to think this is my best angle!"

A Rodian Profile • Another LEGO® *Star Wars*® minifigure close-up, this time lit from above. I figured a profile would do Greedo justice instead of shooting from the front. Like many of my portraits, this was shot against black cardboard for added dramatic effect.

>> Pages 20–1 **The Burnout** • In *The Empire Strikes Back*, Han Solo says "Let's hope we don't have a burnout" to Chewie as they are about to take off from Hoth in the *Millennium Falcon*. The idea here was to show a burnout, with plenty of smoke.

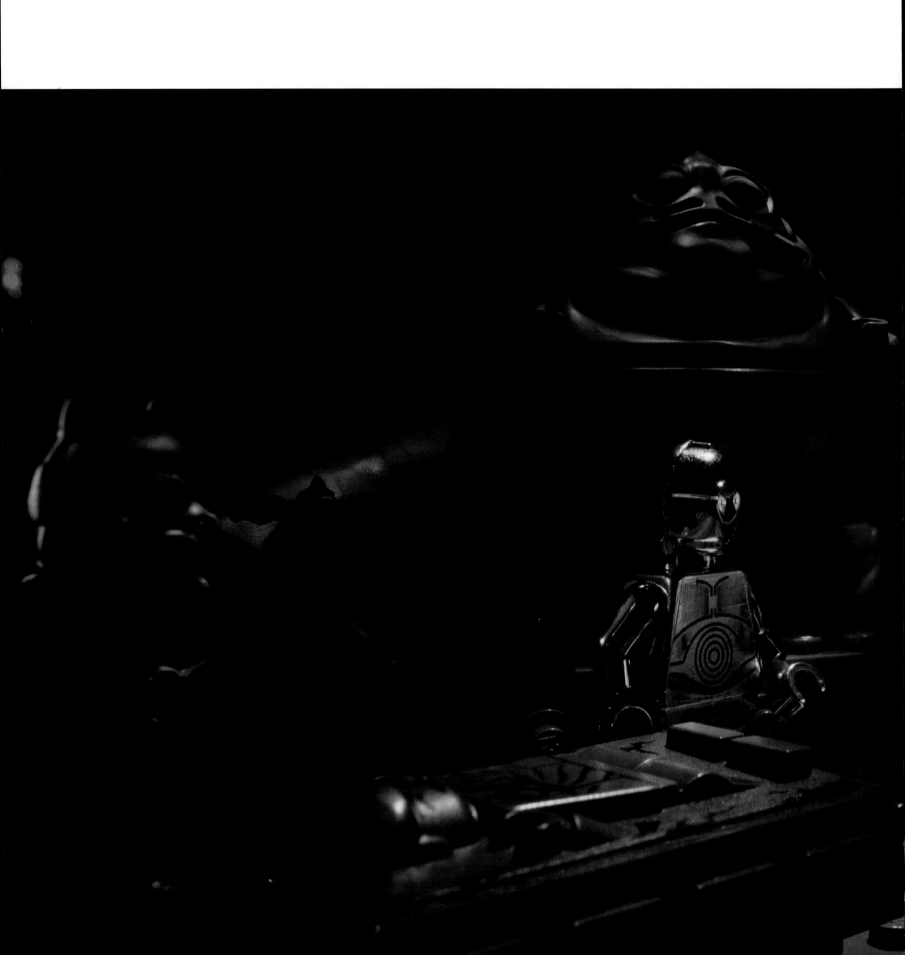

Jabba's Prize • This is a composite image made up of several shots to control the areas of "hot" and "cold" lighting. I imagined that Jabba was unhappy with the condition of his prize possession—Han Solo in carbonite—and ordered bounty hunters Boba Fett, Bossk, and IG-88 to make some repairs.

"We seem to be made to suffer. It's our lot in life."

Goldenrod Portrait • One of the most iconic faces in the *Star Wars* universe belongs to C-3PO. Looks great as a LEGO minifigure, too.

"Mighty Jabba, I bring you gifts!"
"I have no need for exotic birds, bounty hunter."

The First Attempt • The rebels had talked about ostracizing Jabba from his band of hoodlums to create confusion before resucuing Solo, and Princess Leia had confused the words "ostracize" and "ostrich" (not the brightest of puns, I know)… Another composite image of murky goings-on at Jabba's palace, this was one of the first photographs where I used thick smoke for atmosphere. After a while, the smoke got too much and I badly needed a face mask.

"I'm a lot better looking under this mask!"

A Boushh Portrait • Like many of my portraits, this one uses careful lighting to pick out the character's distinguishing features.

"I'll get you for this, Salacious Crumb!"

The Joker of the Northern Dune Sea • Salacious Crumb is an evil little thing and enjoys opening the sliding door over the rancor's pit! To get this image, I placed the LEGO set on a support and the camera on the floor.

"Who are you calling piggy?"

A Gamorrean Portrait • The LEGO *Star Wars* minifigures with unique head sculpts work really well as portraits.

"Hey! Give me back my helmet!"

Rancor's Pit Trooper • I imagined that this trooper TK-24/7 got all the best jobs—like searching the rancor's pit for the stolen plans of the Death Star... It took a while to get the lighting sorted out for this image, I must say... I called the stormtrooper TK-24/7 to convey that he is on duty 24 hours a day, seven days a week.

>> Pages 36–7 **Rancor's Sandpit** • The idea behind this shot was that the attacks of the wild rancors of Tatooine were mostly for show. Just don't move and you're safe! Our local sand is granite-based and too abrasive for LEGO bricks. I used ordinary cornflour and dropped a handful of it as I took the picture. However, it's more difficult to get light to reflect off cornflour, unlike real sand.

"I'm ready for my close-up!"

Jabba the Hutt • This image is lit from below and echoes moody still portraits from classic Hollywood movies, as of Boris Karloff in *Frankenstein* (1931).

"Who cares about the droids—which way is our base?"

Lost in a Midnight Sandstorm • My original idea was to shoot this with direct back lighting. When it didn't work out that well, I moved the camera sideways and noticed a nice lens flare. With only minor adjustments, this is what I got and the result is way better than my original idea.

"All this sand is slowing down my speeder!"

Sand Speeder Bike With Sand Scout • After unsuccessfully trying to shoot speeder bikes on many occasions among plants and trees, I decided to shoot one on sand. Finally, I was able to make them look good.

The Ice-Cream Heist • I imagined that the Jawas might distract Jabba's guards with ice cream in order to steal Jabba's skiff… My first attempt at this was not a success and ended up in my "fails" folder. I later re-edited it and added the sun. The Jawas' yellow eyes were added later from an over-exposed frame.

"Good evening. Can I interest you in our new ice-cream promotion?"

>> Pages 46–7 **A Jawa Finds Trouble** • The Jawa did not know that the lone, hovering droid was an Imperial Probe Droid—very dangerous... I had difficulties shooting the original LEGO Sandcrawler, but the new version works particularly well.

"It's so dark I can't see where the restraining bolt goes!"

Their Last Catch of the Day • This was an early test with the old sandcrawler (set 10144). The idea was to have the treads in the background with the action in front lit from between the treads where the doorway should be. I wanted a sandstorm effect, but it didn't look good and I ended up uploading a very darkly lit version instead. You can't really see the sandcrawler at all.

"I've got a funny feeling I'm being watched!"

Bad News Jawa • I substituted cornflour for sand for this image of a Jawa unearthing an Imperial Probe Droid, and it worked well.

>> Pages 50–1 **The Trouble With the Sandcrawler** • It occurred to me that the Jawas' sandcrawler would have had a large workshop for repairing whatever the Jawas found, but the restroom facilities would be limited and would often malfunction. So the Jawas would have to use the facilities at the Mos Eisley Cantina. The "moon" is a slide-projector slide with a round hole in the center of it. See page 159 for the set-up.

Treat the Treads Well • The idea for this image was that
a Jawa was trying to fix a broken tread on his sandcrawler,
but the WED treadwell droid misunderstood its instructions
and the sandcrawler's treads suddenly fell off.

"Oh dear! This could be a long night!"

"We're the most sinister bounty hunters ever!"

The Bounty Hunters • This image of Bossk and Boba Fett minifigures features the Han Solo carbonite brick in the background—although it is largely obscured by smoke.

Opposite page **Boba Fett's Wonderful Return** • Suddenly, one stormy night on Tatooine, Mr. Fett rises from his sandy tomb... This is a peculiar image for me. Sometimes you have an idea for a shot and it doesn't really work, but you upload it anyway. And people liked it a lot. I was so surprised. Of course this also works the other way. Sometimes I'll upload a picture that I think is really cool and people just say, "Oh, it's okay..."

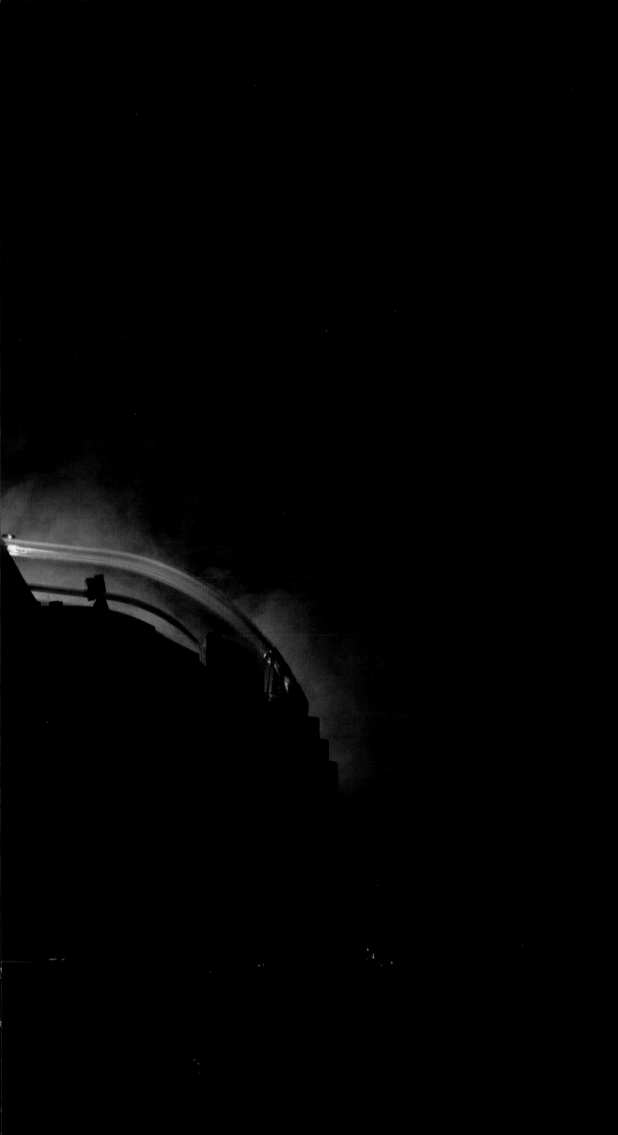

"I always make a dramatic entrance."

The Master of First Impressions •
I imagined that, for an interstellar
bounty hunter like Boba Fett, a
landing platform could be the only
place to make that all-important
awesome first impression. He might
wait hours—days—for the perfect
lighting and weather.

HOTH

This world of ice, snow, and strange beasts is the rebels' secret sanctuary —until they hear that Imperial snowtroopers, led by Darth Vader, are about to attack. The rebels flee Hoth, and the snowtroopers have to find new ways to keep themselves busy.

"Let's take off before it starts snowing again."

X-Wing Dawn Patrol • It proved to be really difficult to get both fighters in the same photo so I had to make some compromises. The outdoor snow field illusion is not perfect in this image, but the fighters look gorgeous.

"Every time he takes off, I get covered!"

High Speed Snowspeeder Flyby • The snowspeeder is angular and therefore I figured it must create major turbulence and draft behind it when flying at speed. I wanted to capture a lot of snow up in the air along with the surface-skimming speeder.

"I'll show you how low I can go!"

Low-Altitude Snowspeeder Patrol Flight • It's difficult to capture speed without the image looking like a static object on a blurred, Photoshopped background. My aim of creating a physical-effect setup spectacular required a proper studio room and assistance. This capture is from a simplified version of the idea and works well. It's an in-camera image with just a couple of fishing lines removed in Photoshop.

"Next time, I'm driving!"

The Crash • Sometimes I like to roam the archives for things I have not noticed. This is one of those. In the original, from August 2010, there are two spectators on the left, witnessing the crash, which is a training flight gone wrong. I wanted to see if this worked on its own. I think the snow here is soft enough to just make the speeder go thump and leave the pilots with snow on their goggles.

"Guys, the weather is really bad today. Let's take the day off."

Briefing on Hoth • I was going for a more movie-like shot with this one. Some of the minifigures kept tipping over in the shallow snow. At some point I did not bother to clean them any more and decided to shoot them as they were. The snow on the minifigures seemed natural—after all, they *are* in a blizzard.

To Catch a Tauntaun • I'm happy with this photograph. It worked beautifully and I had very little to fix in Photoshop. The room I shot this in, however, was all white after I had created a baking powder blizzard with a hairdryer. In fact, virtually our entire apartment was white because I had forgotten to close the doors behind me. This is the messiest photoshoot I've ever had.

"This tauntaun seems almost tame!"

"Ride that tauntaun!"

Breaking in the Tauntaun • The concept behind this image was that the tauntauns, indigenous to Hoth, had to be broken in by a special group of wranglers before the rebels could use them as mounts. The breaking-in process was short but very fierce... I had a definite idea of how the tauntaun should gallop in thick snow and I shot it twice, but couldn't get it right. Getting the snow spray to look right was difficult, but when cropped square, the problem went away nicely. Now, with the colors tweaked, this image feels pretty much perfect. This is how LEGO® tauntauns gallop in thick snow.

"What do you mean, it's behind me?"

Chewie's Bad Day • When I shot this in 2009, Chewbacca was not often photographed, so I thought I'd give it a try. For some reason, I totally blew the first two sessions before I tried this set-up.

"Aarrooogh!"

Chewbacca Portrait • I wanted to show Chewie appearing from a dark doorway, as if you were seeing him for the first time. The current LEGO minifigure of Chewbacca, with its realistic, sculpted head, is so much easier to light effectively and shoot. I tried to take a portrait of the previous Chewie minifigure, but the lack of features made it difficult.

Last Ship to Rendezvous Point •
I imagined that there was no time
for pre-flight checks when the rebel
troops fled their secret base on Hoth.
Under fire from Imperial troops, a
Y-wing fighter took off without its
astromech unit on board. This is one
of my favorite images—it was much
easier to shoot than I ever expected.

" Where have all the rebels gone? "

Hoth: The Dawn After • After seeing a beautiful midwinter sun
outside, I wanted to see if I could create something like it,
so I shot this image. It showed that the Rebel Alliance's
presence on Hoth was over and only destroyed snowspeeders
remained. I must have inhaled a ton of baking powder doing this!

"Hey! I'm walking here!"

The Steps of a Walker • I imagined that the walkers' heavy feet pounding the ground would send tremors kilometers ahead. During the assault on Hoth, many of the snowtroopers were so confused by the noise and vibrations they were nearly stepped on.

"WOW! That's gotta be the best one yet!"

Ka-Boom! • I wanted to use all my snowtroopers in one shot. I decided that they could be investigating the rebel base and accidentally causing explosions. Luckily, the abundance of snow, together with the snowtroopers' armor, would render the explosions harmless.

"Watch where you scoop for snowballs!"

The Thing • I imagined that wampas like to hide in snowdrifts, so that they can make surprise attacks. This was a very quick idea. I just piled powder on a LEGO wampa.

"Gives me a warm glow just looking at it!"

Above **Silent Night, Hothian Night** • This picture features snow lanterns. Finnish kids build them by making a pile of snowballs and putting a candle inside. I made mine with modeling clay and a small lightbulb. I wanted to include snow lanterns in my Hoth pictures because of the contrast their warm light provides with the snow.

Opposite page **The Big Freeze** • With the rebels gone, there was very little happening on Hoth, apart from the occasional wampa. This is the first time I included clouds—made from cotton wool.

"Arooo-eeoo!"
"Yep, certainly brightens the wilderness up!"

Call of the Wild • I always thought of this as a homage to the old Jack London stories, hence the name "Call of the Wild." I used a projection of a sickle-shaped moon here, perhaps conveying a bit of a fairytale feel.

"Now what shall we sing?"

Moonlight Shadow • The idea behind this image was that the snowtroopers often built snow lanterns during nocturnal AT-AT maintenance shifts on Hoth. They considered it an art form. Unfortunately, snow lanterns don't give any heat.

"Captain—I think we've reached tipping point!"

Things That Go Bump in the Night • The walker was suspended on a tilted angle and I just shot the image as I poured powder over it with a spoon.

"That's one feisty little wampa!"

The Bigger They Come, the Harder... There's Three of Them? •
The problem with the wampas was their attitude. They were always looking for a fight... I planned to do a more elaborate shoot, but the first version worked so well that I didn't proceed.

"Silly me! Forgot the ladder!"

A Pilot's Dream •
For this shot, I imagined that a pilot who had never seen snow before took his TIE fighter down, climbed out, and touched snow for the first time. He even built a snow lantern.

The Ice • Trooper TK-24/7's missions had taken him to many planets, including Tatooine, Endor, and Hoth; each planet's environment required different gear. On a routine night patrol on Hoth, TK-24/7's AT-ST walker became stuck in snow. He got out to free it and found a valley of huge ice cubes… The ice is novelty ice cubes made of plastic. I make the baking powder fly like snowflakes by blowing as I take the picture. Baking powder is horrible stuff to inhale, so I haven't done many pictures like this lately.

"These beautiful blocks of ice are strangely inspiring…"

"**I'm getting an idea…**"

The Sub-Zero Inspiration, 1 and 2 • The ice particles that seem to be flying as the sculpture takes shape are pieces of rock salt, which I dropped at the same time as I took the shot. The tiny particles needed to be caught mid-air as they fell. This image needed fast exposure and a lot of attempts to catch the right fraction of a second.

>> Pages 102–3 **The Art of the Frigid Plains of Hoth** •
Introducing the wampa, the biggest indigenous beast of the planet
captured in an amazing ice sculpture by the extremely talented
TK-24/7. For this, I made a rubber mold of a LEGO wampa and
created my ice wampa from acrylic resin. The result was missing a
finger or two, and I had to glue the tusks back on but, as it's
supposed to be an ice sculpture, it didn't have to look perfect.

Ghost in the Machine • I imagined that, because there was so little for the snowtroopers to actually do on Hoth, they decided to hold a Big Freeze festival, with tables, chairs, etc. all made from ice. The idea behind this shot was that a droid had deviated from its instructions to move blocks of ice to the festival site and had made a sculpture of a humanoid. The simple machine had created art.

"Poor little droid. Frozen stiff!"

The Trouble With the Probe Droids • The idea here was that probe droids didn't work well on snowy Hoth nights, and in the morning the snowtroopers had to dig them out. This is one of my earlier snow tests in which I used talcum powder.

" Ha! Ha! Missed again! "

Bullet Time on Hoth •
The idea of a rebel and an Imperial stormtrooper having a day without war and a snowball fight instead appealed to me... A little Photoshopping was required for the snowball, in order to erase a tiny piece of supporting rod. This image was shot in water so that the "snow" fell slowly—like the particles in a snow globe souvenir. It was the first time I got this snow effect to work.

"Wait 'til Darth Vader sees this!"

Ski Trooper • When the LEGO® Minifigures series delivered a pair of white skis in August 2010, I came up with this pretty fast. This was one of the early experiments with different powders tossed around with spoons, spatulas, and whatnot. At this stage, I had decided baking powder was by far the best substitute for snow in miniature scale. I haven't changed my opinion yet.

"The planet Hoth is the *only* ski resort for the serious skier."

The Snowtrooper Big Air • This is a very big
(15000 pixels wide) picture made up of a number
of individual snowtrooper images. This is the closest
to LEGO animation that I have managed.

"Thank the dark side I remembered to wear cosy pajamas under my armor!"

Living in the Dark Side—with Style • I think the snow effect came out nice in this one. I wanted to make it look as if Darth's cape had seen plenty of action.

"Hmm… my Hoth snowtroopers clearly have hidden talents!"

The Ewok Popsicle • I made the ice sculpture Ewok using a rubber mold and acrylic resin.

>> Pages 116–7
Three Kings • The scenario for this was that Darth Vader couldn't see anything with his helmet on as night fell on Hoth, so he had to use his lightsaber as a flashlight… The red light on the walker is actually an accidental reflection of the lit-up lightsaber effect. I left it in because it looked good. The red light on the foot next to the lightsaber, however, is intentional.

Powdered! • I originally intended to have Boba Fett in the picture —the bad guys having a day off—but it didn't work, so I replaced him with the three snowtroopers who witness Darth Vader's skiing mishap. The rough sketch for this image is on page 163.

"Skiing is just a piece of caaaaaaaaaaaake!"

"I've got the baddest ship in the whole galaxy!"

Boba's Ride • I saw the original filming model of Boba Fett's *Slave I* spaceship in the *Star Wars* Identities exhibition in Paris. I was blown away by how fantastic it looked. *Slave I* is great on screen, but looks even better in real life. The LEGO Ultimate Collector's Series *Slave I* captures the shape of the model really well. It's big, heavy, almost intimidating. I like it a lot. I tried to make it look mean and menacing, perhaps reaching for some of the evilness of the original.

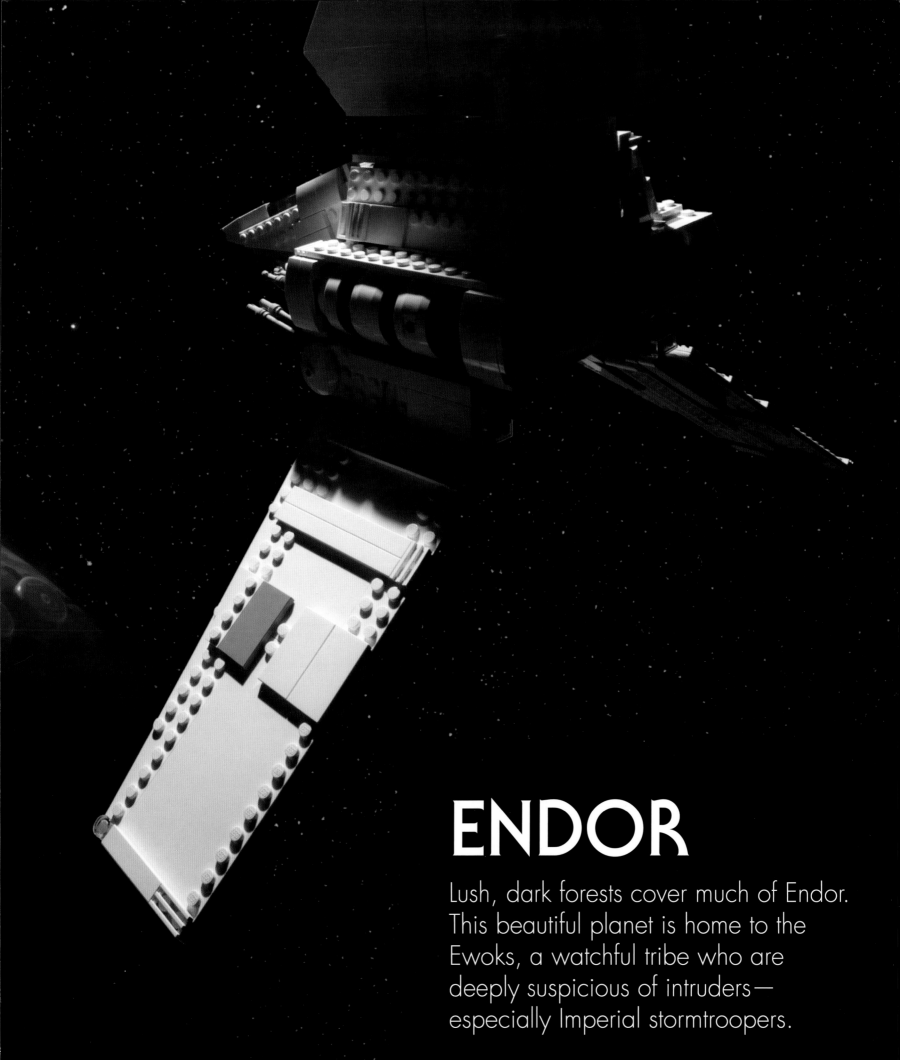

ENDOR

Lush, dark forests cover much of Endor.
This beautiful planet is home to the
Ewoks, a watchful tribe who are
deeply suspicious of intruders—
especially Imperial stormtroopers.

"The beautiful Endor forest is a pleasure to patrol."

Early Morning Scout Patrol • Photographing this was far from being peaceful. It was a very hot day in the woods, very hot! I was sweating hard and being attacked by an army of mosquitoes. That was before I realized I was crouching on a piece of rock hosting some aggressive, biting ants. I created the atmosphere of mist and sunbeams by burning a little tissue paper and blowing the smoke over the minifigure.

"What was that noise?"

Early Morning on Endor • I found the plant in this picture in our backyard. It had accidentally been left outside for the whole winter. Although most of the plant had died, it still had some green on it, so I kept it, thinking it might come in useful.

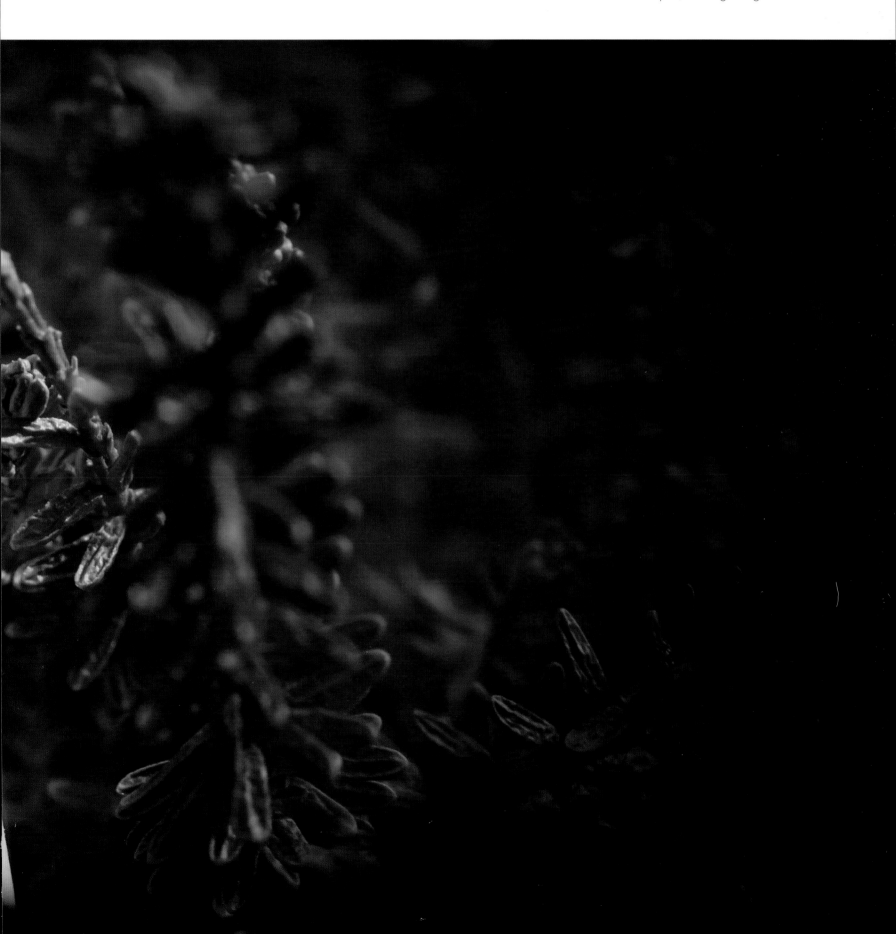

" I could have sworn I heard something… "

Bad to the Bone • This turned out to be an important photograph. Apparently, it caught the attention of the makers of THE LEGO® MOVIE™, who were interested in the way that I had used smoke from burning paper tissue to create atmosphere in a series of photographs. In fact you can just see ashes from the tissue on the heads of the Ewok minifigures.

" Yikes! Face to face with an Ewok! "

The Ewoks of Endor • This was the first time I got the Ewok face to work
in a shot. I had tried to photograph these little rascals several times,
simple portraits, action shots, and whatnot, without success. I shot some
250 frames with different lighting setups, some with natural sunlight.
Sometimes it just takes a little extra work to get a good image.

"Something about this place puts me in a bad mood!"

The Walker in the Woods • The tree stump on which I planned to shoot this, was basking in sunlight when I set up the shot. Then the sun moved. As passersby watched, I stood in a bush next to a LEGO® AT-AT walker waiting for the sun to come back. It didn't. There was another treestump a few meters away, so I heaved the AT-AT on top of it, threw the rebel minifigure on, and fired my camera as fast as I could—and the sun went behind a tree. The Earth revolves too fast.

"Captain—there's a funny little furry creature staring at us."

The Goliath Falls • This was an early experiment with smoke effects. In the foreground is real moss on top of a tree stump, on which I positioned the Ewok minifigure. I don't usually shoot minifigures from the back—perhaps I should do it more often!

"Eee chop yub nub!
[We got freedom!]"

An Ewok Portrait • I particularly like the LEGO
Ewok minifigure's expression—a blank canvas you
can easily project emotion on.

" I bet you blink first! "

An Ewok Encounter • The Ewok stare spelt trouble for many rebels on the Endor moon… I spotted some fresh basil in our kitchen and thought it would look nice as an Endor background. Two minifigures and one hour later I returned the basil to the kitchen unharmed. Household items standing in for galactic locations—I like it!

Opposite page **Ewok Portrait** • An Ewok stares out of the darkness of the Endor Forest.

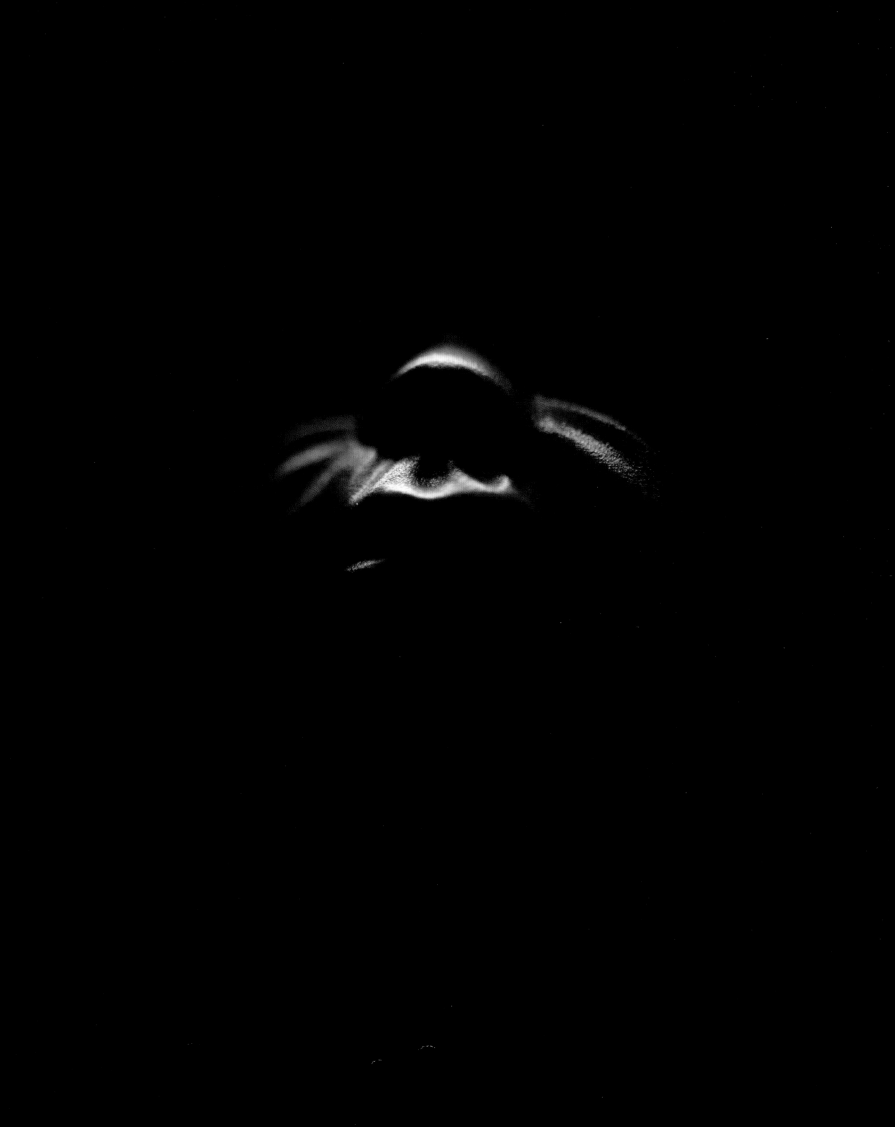

"Funny—my Jedi training tells me there's someone close by…"

The Great Endortrainer • The "Endor" in this shot is our front yard lavender shrub. This was shot late in the evening because I wanted to light it with my slide-projector light for better control. I had a hard time with the focus, though, as the camera was sitting on the lawn. I got twigs and grass in my ear.

"A lost helmet. I've got a bad feeling about this."

Another Helmet Lost on Endor • This helmet is not supposed to belong to anyone in particular. I took this with my old camera, using a 60mm lens. I wanted to experiment with shooting a small object up close.

>> Pages 142-3 **The Ewok Jam** • For this image, I imagined that the Ewoks were a musical lot, always playing and having a good time. Figrin D'an of the Modal Nodes was happy to go to Endor and jam with the Ewoks. The teddy bear (from the LEGO® Minifigures series) is supposed to be a baby Ewok!

"I'm here to jam with those cool cats the Ewoks!"

A Bith Portrait • "Fiery" Figrin D'an is the leader of the band the Modal Nodes. I kept the same setup that I already had for the C-3PO photograph on page 24. These are surprisingly fun to shoot.

The Endor Moon • The experiment here was perhaps
putting branches across the moon. I was initially
disappointed, but I am happy with the photograph now.

"Coatee cha chiutatal!
[Celebrate the moon!]"

Endorian Autumn • Little known fact: the forest moon of Endor had seasons. The Ewoks' mental state followed the cycle and fall was the time for melancholy. It lasted mere hours—the melancholy, that is…

>> Pages 150–1 **The Thing With Old Machines** • I had the idea that the BTL-A4 Y-wing starfighter was fast enough for bombing runs but prone to overheating at full throttle. Landing to cool off the engines would be one way to deal with the problem.

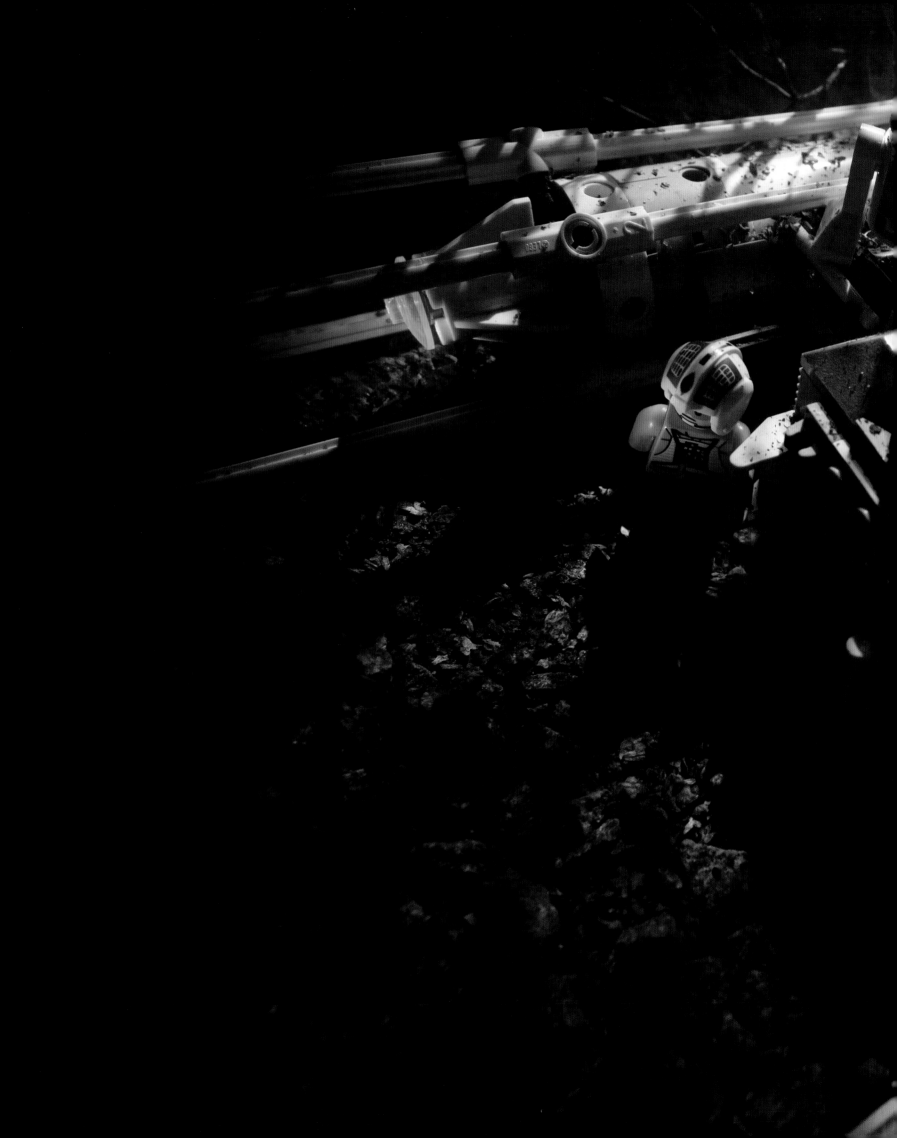

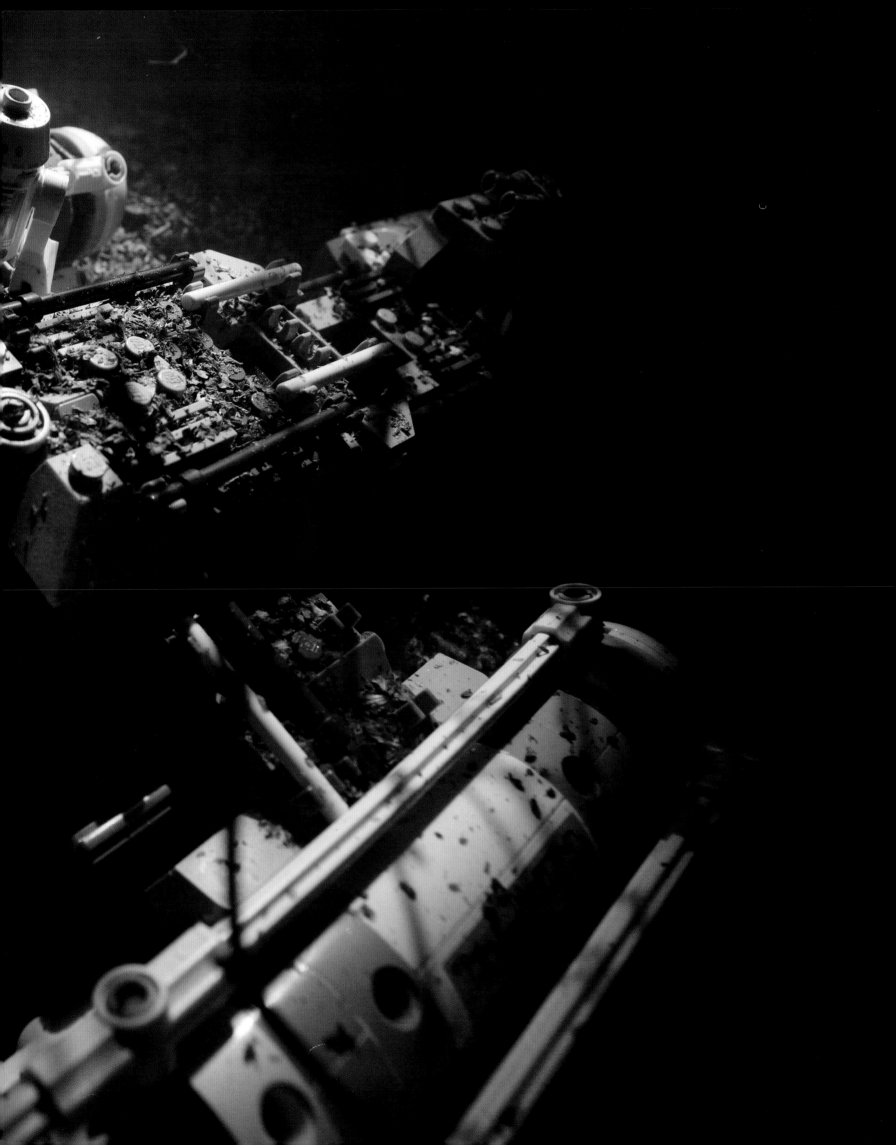

"Coatee cha siz!
Coatee chaeekeekeek!
[Celebrate the fire!
Celebrate the forest!]"

Ewok in the Ashes • Maybe the Endor Forest flourishes if you burn little bits to refresh it! This is a quickly improvised shot. I was preparing dinner in our barbecue and noticed that the charcoal at the bottom of the grill looked great. So I placed that Ewok minifigure in the ashes. Inspiration can strike at any time!

>> Pages 154–5 *Millennium Falcon* • This shows the *Millennium Falcon* under attack from Imperial TIE fighters. I shot it against a white background spray-painted black that I turned into a negative image to convey outer space. The laser effect is a composite image. The warm glow on the TIE fighter is another separate element, achieved through special lighting.

BEHIND THE SCENES

There is much, much more than meets the eye to Vesa Lehtimäki's LEGO® *Star Wars*® photographs. In the following pages, Vesa himself reveals what the *Star Wars* saga means to him, the artists and movies that have inspired him, the equipment he uses and some of the brilliantly simple techniques he employs to create his unforgettable gallery of images.

Studio setup • I have a small studio in my basement. The LED torches are used for some lighting effects. Resting my projector on a stack of books allows me to adjust the height easily.

Opposite page The sandcrawler • In order to accomplish a Tatooine photoseries, I needed the LEGO *Star Wars* Sandcrawler (set 10144). I bought one second-hand. It arrived covered in dust, sticky, and smelly. I washed and scrubbed every single brick, all 1669 of them. It took me almost a week.

> "That is the essence of *Star Wars*' appeal for me—the design."

What is your earliest memory of the *Star Wars* saga?

I saw the first *Star Wars* film shortly after the Finnish premiere in December 1977. I am just another victim of that movie; it changed everything! I don't know why my parents didn't worry about my obsession. Or maybe they did, and they just didn't tell me.

What does *Star Wars* mean to you now?

I have a hard time putting what *Star Wars* means to me into words. It's not just something I was a fan of, I grew up with it. Its influence is deep in me and it's not going to go away. This influence is not so much derived from the characters or from the storylines, but stems from the amazing worlds created for them. That is the essence of *Star Wars*' appeal for me—the design.

Do you have a favorite *Star Wars* film and/or character?

I have especially fond memories of the first two movies, *Star Wars: Episode IV A New Hope* (1977) and *Star Wars:* Episode V *The Empire Strikes Back* (1980). Of course, that has a lot to do with the age I was when I saw them.

The *Star Wars* characters are great, of course, but they aren't my favorite thing about the movies. For me, the true treasures of the saga are the set designers, prop makers, visual artists and model makers— Ralph McQuarrie, Joe Johnston, Roger Christian, John Dykstra, Grant McCune, Lorne Peterson, and the people at ILM (Lucasfilm Ltd.'s visual effects division). Their achievements have not dated at all. The X-wings they conceived and created—and the Y-wings— are just as fantastic as they were almost 40 years ago.

Have you always loved LEGO® sets? What was your first set?

There's a box of LEGO® bricks in our basement. I went through it to refresh my memory and, sure enough, I found some bricks I could connect to the earliest memories of what I played with. I remembered two sets, I looked them up and they turned out to be a delivery truck (set 333 from 1967) and an ambulance (set 373 from 1971). I still have most of the parts of the ambulance; the doors with a red cross, the headlight brick, the wheels.

I built a lot when I was a kid; a LOT! I haven't built since I grew up, though—I just find LEGO models fascinating to photograph.

What led you to create your own LEGO® *Star Wars*® images?

I bought my first DSLR—a Canon 450D, I now have a Canon 5DMK2—for an illustration

" I just find LEGO models fascinating to photograph. "

assignment in 2008 or 2009. Once the assignment was done, in the spring of 2009, I began pointing the camera at toys. My plan was simply to document my son's toys, to create a souvenir photobook of childhood toys for him before they were given away or just vanished.

In July 2009, I uploaded some *Star Wars* action figure photographs to Flickr to try out the platform and I found it very interesting. I then photographed some LEGO *Star Wars* snowtroopers in snow. The feedback was wonderful.

What was the first LEGO *Star Wars* image you took—and have you revisited it?

This is a complicated question, there is no simple answer. My oldest surviving toy photograph is from 1979 or 1980. It's a photo of a Y-wing fighter. I made that model about 19 years before the first official

LEGO Y-wing fighter set. I have since photographed LEGO Y-wings several times but only using official sets. If I have to pick my favorite spaceship from all the *Star Wars* movies, this would probably be it. Sadly, I never had the beautiful big LEGO Ultimate Collector's Series Y-wing set. It was discontinued years before I even knew about it.

I took up photographing toys again in 2009. The first LEGO photograph that I put online was an image of a stormtrooper minifigure running towards the camera. The stormtrooper was photographed inside a plastic, water-filled soda bottle with the top cut off. The reason for this was clear in the next photographs I uploaded, which used the same setup but with a laser beam shooting from one of the stormtroopers' blasters. It's a real laser beam, and a water-based technique I had explored earlier with some *Star Wars* action figures.

The first of many • This photo was taken in 1979 or 1980, simply to capture my own version of a LEGO Y-wing model.

What drew you to photography as an art form? Have any photographers influenced you?

Illustration used to be a hobby, a sideline to my day job as a designer and an art director for magazines. In 2006 I jumped out of the designer's chair and pursued a career as an illustrator. As the pencil became my main tool, illustration stopped appealing as a hobby. I needed a new hobby and the camera fitted the bill perfectly.

I think as an illustrator but work with a camera—I guess that shows in my attempts to control the various elements in each photograph, such as the lighting and aerial manipulation of pieces. In photography, these are often just tools to get the photo done, rather than an organic part of the process as in an illustration. For me, they are quite important.

Some of my influences are from painting and from photography, but by far the biggest is the cinema. I used to watch lots of movies, and movies have made a profound impression on what I do. In fact, I sometimes use the 2.35:1 Cinemascope aspect ratio in my photos because that is the format in which I learned to look at images.

Other than the *Star Wars* saga, what are your favorite movies and movie directors? Do you think they have influenced you? For example some of your darker images with slanting light recall film noir…

I made movies when I was young. Super-8 film was my medium; pretty expensive, but the other option was 16mm. So I saved all my money to buy film. My dad didn't let me hack the film port of his camera to produce a widescreen image on Super-8 film.

My movies weren't that good, and I never made it to film school, but I kept my love for cinema. Filmmakers like Howard Hawks, George Cukor, Billy Wilder, and Jacques Tati certainly knew what they were doing. I also love the film noir of the 1940s and 50s. As I watch movies, I am often aware of the cinematography and editing. I love *Lawrence of Arabia* (1962)—that's epic movie-making at its best. Of contemporary filmmakers, I particularly admire Wes Anderson. *The Royal Tenenbaums* (2001) is one of my favorite movies.

Could you give an insight into how you come up with an idea for a particular shot? Does a setting or character suggest a story, or does a story concept come first?

Sometimes I have a strict plan with sketches, sometimes just a vague idea. I love to work both ways. It is very enjoyable to improvise with the camera, seeing if an idea leads to another, and so forth.

What is your working setup? Do you have a dedicated studio, perhaps with sandpits and snow pits and pot plants full of Ewoks?

I'm really low-tech with that stuff. I've shot a number of my photos on our living-room table, sometimes while everyone else was watching TV. The snows and sands are in plastic containers and simply poured over a sheet of cardboard when needed.

I have cleared some room in the basement, made a tiny studio in a corner and mostly shoot there now. The basement is easier to get dark than the living room but harder to clean when the baking powder flies too far off from the setup.

Shooting stormtroopers • I soon found that techniques I had previously used when photographing *Star Wars* action figures worked equally well when capturing minifigures. I shot these ones inside a water-filled bottle.

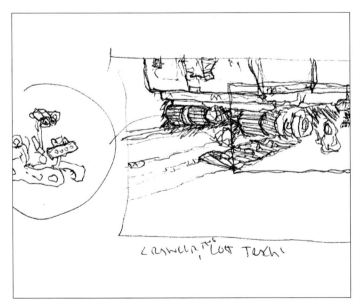

Preliminary sketches • Sometimes I make a small sketch to plan an image before I begin shooting. If I do this, they are generally simple sketches focusing on the basic composition of the shot.

Has your background as an illustrator helped you to formulate your ideas? Do you sketch out an idea first, or simply have an image in your mind?

I have a Master's degree in graphic design, and I've made my living as a designer and illustrator most of my life. I've worked with a lot of talented people and one thing I've learned is not to give up on an idea too easily, and not to settle for good if you're going for best. You can always push an idea a little further.

I have an idea in my mind when I shoot, but I may use sketches to figure out the image first. While shooting I do not look at sketches.

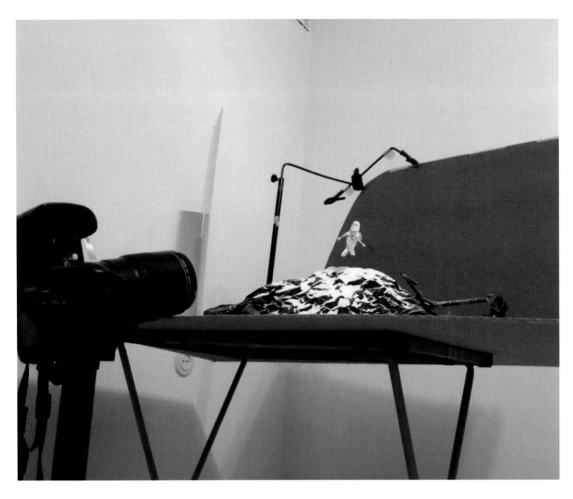

The process • Getting the perfect shot isn't easy. From creating a set and selecting the best camera angle, to cleaning the minifigure between shots—the process can be a long one.

Opposite page Arresting angles • From this angle, sets often look like the toys we are all familiar with. It is only when the camera is placed on the same level, or below, that the scene comes to life.

Your images are full of references to nature. How does the natural world —especially the seasons in Finland and your local environment—inspire your photography?

I love the winter and snow. It can be miserable up here without daylight,

Our light up here is a bit different to more southern parts of the world. Even in the summer, when the sun shines almost 24 hours a day, seven days a week, the light has a cooler tone than it does elsewhere. The air is clear and the clouds float lower than they do in the south.

" When the first snow arrives, I am up and busy with my baking powder in no time. "

and before the snow comes it's just dark and wet. I call it the Mordor season. But nothing beats a good winter's day with snow everywhere and that harsh, cold light you get during the few hours of daylight... It's just beautiful every time.

I love these changes and they certainly inspire my photography. For one thing, I find it very hard to photograph snowy scenes in the summer but when the first snow arrives, I am up and busy with my baking powder in no time.

Arresting lighting is one of your trademarks—do you have any tips that you would like to share?

I like to use stark contrasts and controlled light at times. This is partly due to the fact that I don't know how to light an image otherwise—I don't have a softbox for that smooth, studio look. I learned to photograph toys

Kitchen supplies • It took a few failed attempts for me to refine a technique to portray falling snow.

Final frame • Unaware of the sieve above their heads, the rebels in the finished shot, "The Inconvenient Flaw of the Y-wing" brave a blizzard of ground plaster.

using simple pocket torches, Maglites®, and old desktop lights. I use focused spots of light to bring out the important parts in a photo and leave the unnecessary bits in the dark. To control that I use a black carton with holes, through which I light my subjects. The hole in the carton is great for creating very focused beams of light without spillage.

You are brilliant at using everyday objects to create realistic atmosphere. Can you give some examples of things that you've tried to use and failed with, or had surprising success with?

A blizzard was the first new thing that I attempted to do with LEGO photographs. It had never been attempted when I started and I thought it was a great idea. I tried to create a blizzard with flour at first but it looked terrible. Then I figured that I needed to control the snowfall somehow, to slow it down,

and I thought of those little snow globes you see in souvenir shops. I dug up an old CD storage box, filled it with water, and poured gypsum powder that was ground

> **" I use focused spots of light to bring out the important parts in a photo. "**

from an old mold with a cheese grater. It didn't work very well at first, as you can tell from the full title of one of my photos: "Guys? Hey, guys? This ain't funny! Guys, where are you? HELLO?" [*see page 2*]. In it, the powder is just white mush. I got the hang of the snow effect soon, though, and got it to work pretty well.

The CD box was small and, when I wanted to create larger vistas, I needed to either buy an aquarium or work out how to shoot snow dry. I went for dry. I tested with baby powder but it had no sheen. Powdered sugar was a horribly sticky mess to work with. I hated it.

Then I read somewhere that the *Star Wars* visual effects team had used baking soda for the *Empire Strikes Back*'s Hoth miniature scenes. I wanted to try it, but there was only baking powder in our kitchen. However baking powder has soda in it, so I tried that instead. It was perfect, better than soda at the small scale I wanted to use it.

However, despite my success with baking powder for snow, I have never been truly happy with the materials I have used for sand in my photographs. That still needs work.

What has been the hardest shot ? Is there "one that got away?"

I have a folder on my computer that

has fails in it. These are images that I did not like and decided to save for another attempt later. There may be ones that "got away", but I have not given up on any of them yet, so I really can't tell.

"Breaking in the Tauntaun" [see page 70] took four years and two photoshoots to get right. I first shot it in 2010, but I was never really happy with it. Another attempt a year later with another camera gave better results but there was still something that bugged me. In 2014, I was preparing a third shoot of the same idea and went through the frames from the second shoot (I save all my data from the shoots) and I found the perfect frame. Cropping it to a square format really made it stand out and I never proceeded to a third shoot. I don't think I can improve on this one.

Are some LEGO minifigures easier to shoot than others? Do you have a favorite?

I think they are all difficult, but the ones with sculpted head pieces or helmets are a bit easier because there are features you can work with using lights and reflections.

> ❝ "Breaking in the Tauntaun" took four years and two photoshoots to get right. ❞

Stormtrooper minifigures frequently appear in your work—why is that? Are they particularly adaptable as subjects or is there something about them that particularly attracts/ amuses/inspires you?

There is something very amusing about the stormtrooper minifigure.

But I find the snowtrooper even more amusing. The almost featureless helmet and lack of any head movement somehow reminds me of the deadpan humor of Buster Keaton. Without any facial expression, all the other features stand out more and the positioning of the body, especially the hands, becomes more telling. I find that a very interesting means of delivering a story. Snowtroopers also work well against the whiteness of snow.

Do you have a favorite photo?

I have several, I guess. I like "The Moonlight Shadow" [see page 90] a lot, it captures everything that I'd learned at that time in one lucky exposure.

The image is the last frame of what was a very difficult shoot. I did not get it to work as I had hoped and for the final attempt I just blew on the snow in frustration and dismantled the setup. As I went through the frames, I realized that the last one was the exposure I had been looking for.

Opposite page **Nearly there** • I initially rejected all my shots from two different "Breaking in the Tauntaun" shoots. At the time I was unhappy with what I had produced.

Above **In hindsight** • It was only some years later, when I reviewed my old images in preparation for a new shoot, that I found a shot I was happy with.

I am very pleased with how the snow flies just above the ground next to the troopers by the lantern. It's barely noticeable but adds so much to the atmosphere. This is not a perfect frame, the focus is just a tiny fraction off but I like it nevertheless.

One more favorite is "The Last Ship to Rendezvous Point" [see pages 76–7]. It doesn't look that spectacular, but I recently saw it printed on metallic paper mounted on a huge acrylic plate 115 x 76 cm [45 x 30 in] and the atmosphere of it was just dreamy. I loved seeing it at that size.

Do you have a favorite camera?

Not really. I use a Canon 5DMK2 but any full-sensor camera would do, I guess. I bet a good crop-sensor camera would do just as well, too.

Your work helped to inspire the creators of THE LEGO® MOVIE™ (2014). Can you explain how this came about and your involvement in the making of the film?

One of the production companies behind the movie contacted me. They wanted to talk about how and why I had made my photographs. It turned out that they had examined my photos when they were making LEGO *Star Wars: The Padawan Menace*, but they now wanted to know more about the process in order to help define the visual language of THE LEGO MOVIE.

> " I even coined a term… "The Forced Atmospheric Perspective" effect. "

We had some discussions via email and video chat and I talked them through my photographs. The thing they were most interested in were those photographs that featured subtle smoke effects. At the time, I had realized that there were no photos of LEGO minifigures in which anyone had really explored old filmmaking techniques. By this I mean the classic method of shooting with a small amount of smoke in the air to emphasize the air in a controlled

A vision • Working alone on shoots gives me the freedom to follow my creative impulses during the shoot's progression.

space. I used that with LEGO models and it worked perfectly. I even coined a term for the effect: "The Forced Atmospheric Perspective" effect. I googled it and I didn't find any usage of that term at the time. Those shots had apparently caught the filmmakers' attention.

We talked about Douglas Trumbull's water-tank clouds (*Close Encounters of the Third Kind*) and smoke rooms (*Blade Runner*) and all that. They got the idea and ended up using the same basic idea in the smoke-filled spaces of THE LEGO MOVIE.

This process and my involvement has been discussed in interviews and blog posts by Craig Welsh (lighting supervisor for THE LEGO MOVIE) and Grant Freckelton (production designer for THE LEGO MOVIE).

What advice would you give to anyone keen to photograph their own LEGO collection?

The lesson I learned from the truly talented professional photographers I have worked with is very simple: Don't settle for good, go for better. That is a good maxim for anyone picking up a camera for the first time, as well as an experienced photographer. Push yourself and try to do your best. And whatever you do, don't hold the camera too tight. Have fun with it.

Setup for "The Arrival" • Once a scene is fully established and the models are in place, I can experiment with the positions of minifigures, the lighting, and the camera angle. Sometimes my photographs are not entirely accurate to the world of *Star Wars*. For example, here I have included two moons, while in the movies, Hoth has three.

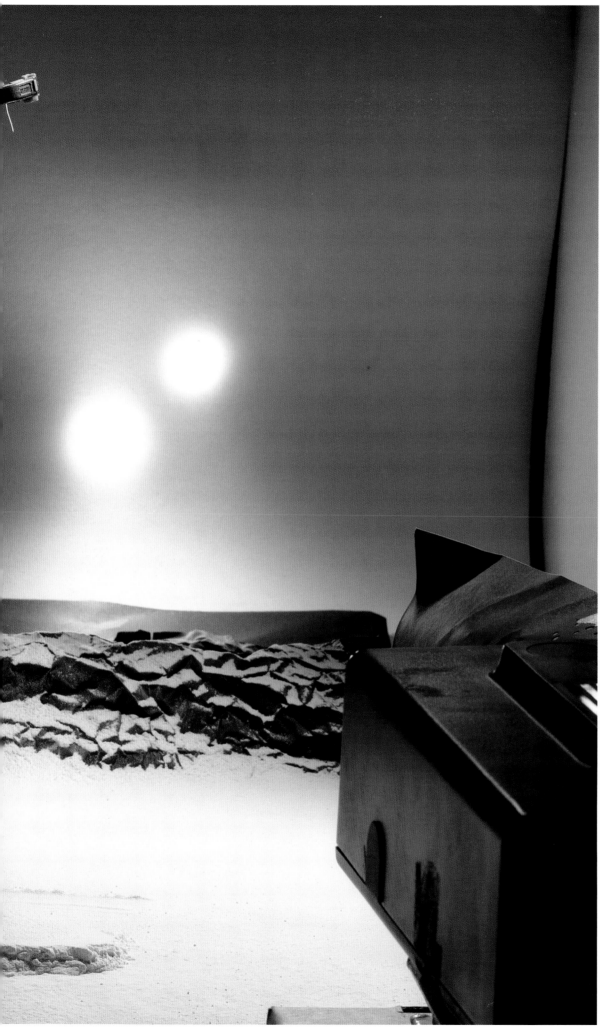

APPENDIX

A list of the key LEGO® Star Wars® sets featured throughout the book.

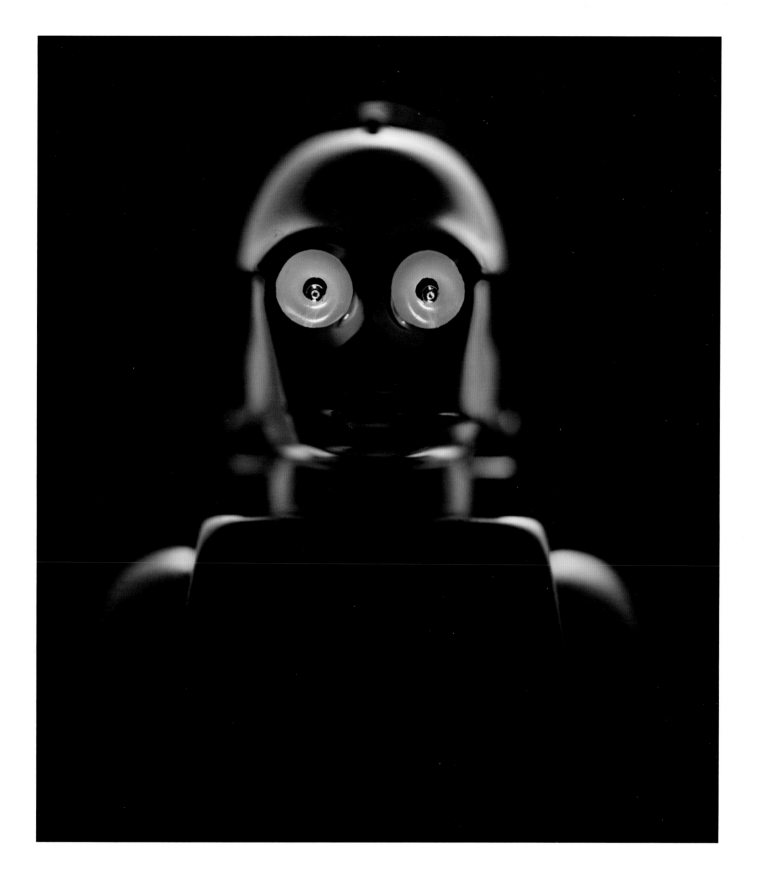

AUTHOR'S ACKNOWLEDGMENTS

My wife, Eeva, thank you for never doubting.

My fellow illustrators: Lasse Rantanen and Ville Tietäväinen, thank you for taking this seriously at the office. Oskari Hellman. My friends at Stuck in Plastic (stuckinplastic.com): Shelly Corbett (@xxsjc), Boris Vanrillaer (@_me2_) and Mike Stimpson (@balakov). Toby Dutkiewicz and all the kind and incredible people at the LEGO Group I have worked with. Everyone involved in making this book at DK, Disney, Lucasfilm, and the LEGO Group, I am still pinching myself! All the people who have commented my photographs online and directly over the years. My parents for letting me be me back then. George Lucas.

Senior Editor Alastair Dougall
Senior Designer Lisa Sodeau
Editorial Assistant Beth Davies
Pre-Production Producer Marc Staples
Senior Producer Louise Daly
Managing Editor Simon Hugo
Design Manager Guy Harvey
Art Director Lisa Lanzarini
Publisher Julie Ferris
Publishing Director Simon Beecroft

Dorling Kindersley would like to thank Randi Sørensen, Paul Hansford,
and Martin Leighton Lindhardt at the LEGO Group, Jonathan Rinzler at Lucasfilm,
and photographer Maarit Kytöharju for the images of Vesa at work.

First American Edition, 2015
Published in the United States by DK Publishing
345 Hudson Street, New York, New York 10014

DK books are available at special discounts when purchased in bulk for
sales promotions, premiums, fund-raising, or educational use. For details, contact:
DK Publishing Special Markets, 345 Hudson Street, New York,
New York 10014
SpecialSales@dk.com

Printed in China

www.LEGO.com
www.dk.com

A WORLD OF IDEAS:
SEE ALL THERE IS TO KNOW